Please Pass

the Salt

Carpenter Ministries
www.carpenterministries.org

Please Pass The Salt

*All Scriptures taken from the
NEW AMERICAN STANDARD BIBLE,
© Copyright The Lockman Foundation 1960, 1962,
1963, 1968, 1971, 1972, 1973, 1975, 1977
Used by permission.*

*Copyright © Carpenter Ministries, 1999
Published by Carpenter Ministries*

*For information regarding other Carpenter
Ministries publications please contact:*

Carpenter Ministries

Web page: www.carpenterministries.org

All rights reserved.

ISBN: 1522795286
ISBN-13: 9781522795285

Dr. Shirley M. Carpenter

CONTENTS

	Acknowledgments	vii
Chapter 1	The Salt Is Between Us	Pg 1
Chapter 2	The Preservative Power Of Salt	Pg 9
Chapter 3	The Covenant Of A King	Pg 19
Chapter 4	A Dinner To Remember	Pg 30
After Thoughts	Is Anyone Thirsty	Pg 44

Dr. Shirley M. Carpenter

ACKNOWLEDGMENTS

What would I ever do without faithful friends? I honestly don't ever want to find out. It is always amazing to see how many people it takes to get even the smallest project accomplished. Once again, I want to take a moment to thank each of you who played a part in completing this work.

Dan Gardner When I received the manuscript you proofed, all nicely decorated with all that red ink, Greg said, "You know, that guy is a real treasure." I heartily agree. Your input was priceless and I believe this booklet is better for it! Thank you once again, faithful friend!

Linda Dircks To "commatize" or not to "commatize", that is the question. I love having you proof my work. Your excitement and enthusiasm make me want to write 100 more. You are a delight! Thanks!

Jim Dube` I agree, I hope we sell a billion also! What a blessing to have a pastor who is also a friend. Thanks again for your help and your encouragement!

Judson Cornwall I always appreciate your input. Your thoughts mean a great deal to me. You are a busy man, and yet you always find time to be a faithful "father." Thank you!

Michele Gillette What a treat it is to work side by side with your own flesh and blood in the business of the kingdom. I couldn't have accomplished this without you dear daughter. Thank you for your willing heart, your encouraging attitude, and best of all, thank you for being my friend!

Greg Carpenter What a gift you are! You are always ready to help out wherever you are needed. You make my life richer in every way and the body of Christ is richer as well! Love you babe!

Dr. Shirley M. Carpenter

INTRODUCTION

Salt is one of those every day, common items we rarely spend much time contemplating. Unless we've been placed on a salt-free diet, it is not normally at the top of our list of significant topics of conversation. But a meal without this savory seasoning would quickly bring our attention to its worthiness.

As we begin to examine this simple mineral, we promptly perceive its importance. With an estimated list of 14,000 uses of this elementary compound of chlorine and sodium, we soon become aware of its indispensability in our everyday lives.

Salt is essential for healthy bodies and is necessary for our cells to live and function. Our lives are often characterized by blood, sweat and tears, all of which contain salt.

Many of the uses of salt seem paradoxical. Salt is used to melt ice, while also utilized to hasten bringing water to the boil. It is a necessary component in refrigeration, and yet used in forging steel.

It has been recognized through the ages for it antiseptic qualities. It was a religious custom of the Hebrews to rub their newborns with it to insure good health.

When an electric current is passed through a salt solution, the salt is divided into caustic soda, or lye which is used for making soaps, washing powders, paper, rayon and to purify petroleum. This electrolysis process also generates chlorine which is used to make paper white and to purify water.

Besides the fact that I love my food on the savory side, salt has played a major part in my personal life. My maiden name means 'salt'. My children were born and raised in the Detroit, Michigan area, a city built on one of the largest salt mines in the United States. And since God said he stores all our tears in heavenly vials, I'm sure I have a few vats full stowed somewhere.

Yet all these attributes, uses and points of importance pale when we look at salt from God's perspective. God put blood and salt in a classification that superseded all others. The truth of God's eternal salt covenant with man has been lost through the ages. I believe it is God's desire to restore the understanding of this tenet to the church and bring healing to the body of Christ.

Chapter 1

The Salt Is Between Us

*All the offerings of the holy gifts,
which the sons of Israel offer to the Lord,
I have given to you and your sons
and your daughters with you, as a perpetual allotment.
It is an everlasting covenant of salt before the Lord
to you and your descendants with you.
Numbers 18:19*

Dr. Shirley M. Carpenter

Chapter 1

The Salt Is Between Us

Commitment Deterioration

Language changes over the years. Meanings of words often mutate. What was once "really hot" is now "really cool" and was once "really tuff". A good example is found in I Peter 3:1-2 in the King James (emphasis is mine).

> *Likewise, ye wives, be in subjection to your own husbands; that, if any obey not the word, they also may without the word be won by the* **conversation** *of the wives; While they behold your chaste* **conversation** *coupled with fear.*

At first glance one might think a woman is encouraged to talk her husband to death, or rather to life, but looking back at the English language in the time of the King James translation, we discover the word "conversation" to actually mean "behavior." She is really being instructed to stop preaching and start living!

Each generation has a way of identifying itself not only with clothes fads, but often in its use of words. What my mom means when she says, "Yeah, right," is quite different than the message my grandkids convey.

The word "commitment" is one of those changing words. Not long ago, it was quite respectable and even desirable to be known as a person of commitment. Today, however, it would seem that commitment is something to be avoided. Couples now live together instead of marrying because they are not willing to make life-long commitments. Unfortunately, our divorce rate shows that those who "take the plunge" by exchanging marriage vows often forsake their commitment when the waters begin to get a little rough. The lack of commitment is also clearly seen in the church world. Believers often hop from church to church looking for a place to fulfill their needs, but often leave as quickly as they came when things don't seem to suit their fancy. It becomes increasingly more difficult to find workers and leaders who will be committed to the work of the church. We tend to be a fickle fraternity that loses interest when things don't go our way, or we become unhappy or disillusioned.

In this world of countless changes, it is reassuring to know that God's concept of commitment remains unaltered. The words of Deuteronomy 7:9 are as sure today as when God breathed them through His servant Moses before the congregation of Israel.

> *"Know therefore that the Lord your God, He is God, the faithful God, who keeps His covenant and His loving-kindness to a thousandth generation with those who love Him and keep His commandments;*

God does more than just make promises; He makes covenants. His word is not merely a declaration that He will or will not do something, it is a binding oath. I'm sure the majority of Christians have heard teachings regarding the blood covenant God made with His people and how it is seen throughout the Word. We are aware of its significance regarding salvation, but are we aware that His commitment goes beyond a covenant of salvation?

In Leviticus 2:13 we read:

> *Every grain offering of yours, moreover, you shall season with salt, so that the salt of the covenant of your God shall not be lacking from your grain offering; with all your offerings you shall offer salt.*

God demonstrated His commitment to His people through a Covenant of Salt, as well as the Blood Covenant. To understand the extent of this pact we need to look back and examine this ancient alliance.

The Salt Covenant

Salt is something we give little consideration today. At thirty-nine cents a box we are assured of having plenty on hand without breaking the bank. But in ancient times, salt held a more prestigious position. It was so highly valued that it was part of the wages of the Roman soldiers, which birthed the old adage,

"A man is worth his salt." Also the phrase, "eating a man's salt" was equivalent to saying you received pay from him. The salt portion of Caesar's Soldiers' pay was called "salarium" or "salt-money" and is the word from which we get our word "salary".

In such a hot climate and in a time when refrigeration was not available, salt played an extremely important part in preserving foods and meats. It was also used to extract the blood from meats. The Law forbade man from eating any blood; therefore the laws were strict in preparation of meat to assure the blood was removed.

After the destruction of the Temple in 70 AD, the table set for a meal was considered an altar. Before the blessing could be recited the salt had to be placed on the table. A meal without salt was considered no meal at all!

Salt was so important to their lifestyle that it was used to ratify covenants. The Salt Covenant became an alliance of friendship. Nations, tribes, neighbors and individuals sanctioned this pact by sitting down at a meal together and partaking of salt contained in the bread. Thus the phrase, "The salt is between us." The covenant bound the partakers to protect one another in times of danger and provide in times of need. When famine or disaster hit, they could turn to their salt-sealed associates to help sustain them. When one nation went to war, they knew they could call on their salt covenant comrades to aid them in their fight.

As a result, the covenant also became known as a Friendship Covenant.

Residue of this covenant still exists in Jewish tradition today. Many Jewish families welcome their new neighbors by bringing a box of salt as a token of friendship.

God's Salt Covenant With Israel

Salt covenants were well known throughout the ancient world. Israel, Egypt and the surrounding nations knew the procedure in making this pact. As a result, Israel was far more aware of God's promises to them than we are in the twentieth (and twenty-first) century. We may know the story, but often miss its substance.

As the children of Israel stood on the threshold of their deliverance, God gave them instructions to prepare for their departure. God was about to take them on the greatest journey of their lifetime, but before they could leave, they had to sit down at a dinner table. The meal did not consist merely of the Passover lamb, but of the prescribed unleavened bread. Knowing there would not be enough time for the leaven to do its work, God ordered them to bake it before it had risen. It was imperative for them to eat bread together at this memorable meal. Why? Because it was more than just giving them strength and sustenance; it even went beyond the promise of their deliverance. God was about to join them at their table and make a salt covenant. Through the shedding of the blood of the lamb He promised them deliverance. In the eating of the bread with its salt He promised them protection and provision on their journey. When the battles would come, He would be there to fight for them. When needs would arise as they traveled through the desert wasteland, He would be there to meet them. He would not merely be their savior; He would be their friend.

Chapter 2

The Preservative Power of Salt

*Know therefore that the Lord your God, He is God,
the faithful God, who keeps His covenant and
His lovingkindness to a thousandth generation
with those who love Him and
keep His commandments.
Deuteronomy 7:9*

Dr. Shirley M. Carpenter

Chapter 2

The Preservative Power of Salt

Salt has been used through the ages for its amazing preservative quality. This attribute is also mirrored in the salt covenant. We can discern God's perception of this property as we look back into Israel's history and observe His reaction to a broken covenant.

After forty years of wandering in the wilderness due to Israel's unbelief, they were finally in the process of possessing the land. They had successfully taken Jericho. They'd fought the battle of Ai twice with an ultimate outcome of victory. It was obvious God was staying true to His friendship covenant with His people. God had instructed them to make no covenants with the inhabitants in the land. They were to annihilate all its residence and take ownership of what He was giving them.[1]

It wasn't long before news got around that the new kid on the block was truly an adversary to fear. The great city of Gibeon which was sure to be the next name on Israel's hit list weighed its options. They came to the conclusion that they were no match for the fearless foe who was relentlessly blazing a victory trail in their direction. The leaders of Gibeon assembled and engaged brains rather than their brawn to insure survival in the land. With old shoes on their feet, worn sacks in their hands and moldy bread in their presumed provisions, a delegation was sent to deceive the elders of Israel. When they arrived in Israel's camp they put on an academy award performance, convincing Joshua and the leaders that they had come from a distant land to make peace with them. They stroked the ego of the Israeli leaders by rehearsing the reports they had heard concerning their impressive success. They even put on a pretense of accepting the God of Israel as the source of their victory. As the men of Gibeon stood with the appearance of pitiful, lost puppies in dire need of protection, the mighty men of Israel responded from their own reasoning's. One quick consultation with God and the Gibeonites would have been exposed. Instead, we are told that when the deceivers held out their hands and said, "This is our bread," Israel's leaders "accepted their provisions."[2] (lit. Hebrew).

Three days later the news broadcast finally came to the camp of Israel and they learned that their neighbors had really pulled one over on them. Joshua and the leaders journeyed to Gibeon to confront them. It didn't matter that this alliance was totally against God's commands, or that it had been ratified through deception; the dastardly deed was done and Israel would have to live with it. Although they allowed the inhabitants of Gibeon to live, they relegated them to a life of servitude as wood choppers and water drawers.[3]

We continue to see this friendship alliance intact when we read about the king of Jerusalem, the king of Hebron, the king of Jarmuth, the king of Lachish and the king of Eglon coming together to attack Gibeon for affiliating with the adversary. Quickly, the men of Gibeon sent word to Joshua and the elders of Israel informing them of their circumstances. The salt covenant required the Israelites to respond as allies. Joshua and the troops marched all night and surprised the opposing kings. God demonstrated His honor of the covenant and led the battle by throwing down hailstones. More died from God's heavenly slingshot than from the swords of the sons of Israel. God went so far as to stop the earth on its axis to give Joshua and the Israelite army more time to soundly defeat their enemies.[4]

We get an even greater glimpse of the strength of this covenant when we follow the trail of Israel's history. Over four hundred years had passed since Joshua and the elders had made the ill-conceived covenant. The days of the judges had ended. King Saul had met his fateful end. David had been reigning in Israel for approximately 33 years and had just come through the sad ordeal of the revolt led by his son, Absalom. After his reign was reestablished, God continued to clean house. David's reinstatement was marked by three consecutive years of famine. Unlike the Israelite leaders in the time of Joshua, David went to God for council concerning the obvious judgment on the land. God's response to him was, *"It is for Saul and his bloody house, because he put the Gibeonites to death."*[5] Saul's zeal for Israel caused him to disregard the friendship covenant Joshua and the leaders had ratified almost 400 years earlier. Man may have felt that time had sapped the strength of the covenant, but the eternal God saw it as eternally binding.

The High Price of Salt

God was not pleased with the broken covenant between Israel and the Gibeonites. David, being a man after God's own heart, immediately took steps to set the record straight. Knowing it was the Gibeonites who had been wronged, David asked them what they felt would be fair to right this wrong.[6] The Gibeonites responded:

> *"We have no concern of silver or gold with Saul or his house, nor is it for us to put any man to death in Israel."*[7]

David assured them this act was under his authority and that they were free to name their price. The Gibeonites then said:

> *"The man who consumed us, and who planned to exterminate us from remaining within any border of Israel, let seven men from his sons be given to us, and we will hang them before the Lord in Gibeah of Saul, the chosen of the*

Lord."8

In today's society, this may seem like a mighty high price. But when we examine it in light of the times it occurred, we find it to be fair, even quite merciful. The Law of God allowed them to rightfully request an eye for an eye and a tooth for a tooth; one life for every life taken. The Gibeonites made it clear to David that they were not seeking revenge, but merely to reestablish the covenant.

The Gibeonites understood the significance of the number seven in Jewish culture. The Hebrew word for "oath" (shebuah) literally means "to seven one's self", or "to bind one's self by oath." Seven is the covenant number. Abraham understood its importance when he met with Abimelech. Abraham informed Abimelech of the ongoing problem of the wells. Abraham's men would dig wells and Abimelech's men would seize them. Abimelech promised Abraham this would not happen again. Abraham removed seven ewe lambs from his flock. When Abimelech questioned the meaning of the seven ewes, Abraham replied, *"You shall take these seven ewe lambs from my hand in order that it may be a witness to me, that I dug this well."*9 That day he and Abimelech made a covenant, and the well became known as Beersheba, "the well of oath" ("beer" meaning "well" and "sheba" meaning "seven").10

The Gibeonites requested that the covenant number of Saul's sons be hung before the Lord in Saul's hometown. Knowing they had requested a fair exchange, David agreed. He added one stipulation to their request; he would not give them Mephibosheth, the son of Jonathan the son of Saul.[11] Unlike Saul, David was a man who understood and honored covenant relationships. David and Jonathan had sealed a friendship covenant and David was determined to keep it.[12]

The designated time Saul's sons were put to death also solidified the reestablishment of the salt covenant. We are told:

> "...and they were put to death in the first days of harvest at the beginning of barley harvest."[13]

Barley harvest was the joyous time when Israel remembered her salt-covenant with God. It was the season all Israel celebrated the Passover and the feast of unleavened bread. As the Israelites sat down to remember the faithfulness of the One who had covenanted to be their protector and provider, the Gibeonites experienced the reinstatement of their treaty with Israel. Once again, God's blessings could rest on His people.

Scripture References

[1] Exodus 23:32-33
[2] Joshua 9:14
[3] Joshua 9

Please Pass The Salt

[4] Joshua 10
[5] II Samuel 21:1
[6] II Samuel 21:3
[7] II Samuel 21:4
[8] II Samuel 21:5-6
[9] Genesis 21:30
[10] Genesis 21:31-32
[11] II Samuel 21:7
[12] I Samuel 18:3 & I Samuel 20:12-17
[13] II Samuel 20:9(b)

Dr. Shirley M. Carpenter

Chapter 3

The Covenant of a King

*Do you not know that the Lord God of Israel
gave the rule over Israel forever to David and his sons
by a covenant of salt?*
II Chronicles 13:5

Dr. Shirley M. Carpenter

Chapter 3

The Covenant of a King

It is no small wonder that God came to David regarding the broken salt covenant. Not only was David familiar with a covenant of friendship through his relationship with Jonathan, he had first-hand knowledge of a salt covenant with God.

II Chronicles 13:5 asks an intriguing question:

Do you not know that the Lord God of Israel gave the rule over Israel forever to David and his sons by a covenant of salt?

One day as I was reading this scripture, I realized my honest answer was, "Why no, I didn't know that!" What a revelation to discover that the eternal reign of the Lion of the Tribe of Judah was promised to David through a salt covenant. But when did this covenant meal take place? Certainly, something this monumental would have been recorded for all times. Someplace, somewhere there had to have been a covenant meal in which God bound Himself specifically to David as protector and provider.

To find the answers we need to go back to the time David fled Saul's palace. David had been the greatest warrior in Saul's army, as well as his great comforter as an instrumentalist. When the army would return from battle, songs were sung in the streets. "Saul has killed his thousands, and David his ten thousands" was the hit of the day. The king became fearful and suspicious of David's success and popularity. He had commanded his servants, as well as his son Jonathan to put David to death. Jonathan stood in the gap and defended David to his father. Saul promised Jonathan that David would not be killed. He called for David to come and soothe his troubled spirit by playing on his harp. But the awareness of God's anointing on David drove Saul into a greater rage. He picked up his spear and hurled it at David, narrowly missing him and driving it into the wall. David quickly slipped out of the enraged presence of Saul. That night David's wife Michal, Saul's daughter, aided David in his escape as she lowered him through the window of their quarters.[1]

David quickly fled to Samuel at Ramah. Saul sent messengers to capture David and bring him back. But the word and the Spirit of God were stronger than Saul and his commands. The envoy found themselves overtaken by the power of God and wound up prophesying in Samuel's presence. Saul sent a second emissary only to have the scene replayed. Saul decided to go himself and do what the others found impossible. Once again, the Spirit of the Lord captured David's enemy and overtook Saul's spirit. Saul ended up prophesying as he came to Samuel. So complete was

Saul's capture that he stripped himself of his royal dignity and laid naked before Samuel as one who was a captive. The fact that he was prophesying as he laid prostrate before him gave clear indication as to who held him prisoner.[2]

David fled Ramah while the Spirit detained his would-be captor. Quickly he made his way to his best friend Jonathan to see if he could shed some light on what it was David had done. Jonathan's great love for David made it difficult for him to believe his father could hate David so much that he would pursue his life. It didn't take long for Jonathan to confirm David's plight and after solidifying the friendship between them, David fled once more.[3]

Because of the haste of his departure, there was no time to gather provisions. David stopped by the Tabernacle at Nob and requested five loaves of bread from Ahimelech the priest. When he asked David why he was alone, David told him that he and his men were being sent on a secret mission of the king and his men were waiting for him in a designated location. Ahimelech related to David that the only bread he had available was the bread on the Table of Shewbread. This bread was consecrated for the priests.

It was at this point David found himself in his direst dilemma. David was fully aware that eating bread set apart for the priests could be his last meal.[4] God didn't take too kindly to those who disregarded His commands and instructions. David was quite familiar with the fate of Nadab and Abihu, the sons of Aaron who went outside the bounds of God's regulations concerning the Tabernacle and its offerings.[5] David considered God's promise that he would someday be king over Israel. His only hope of seeing God's word come to pass was if God acted as his protector and provider. In a blatant act of faith, David instructed the priest to give him the sacred bread.[6] As David ate the covenant bread he forced God to act. Either God would have to kill him for his insubordination or honor the friendship covenant ratified in the salt. If God allowed him to live, He would have to be his keeper . David's unfeigned faith moved the heart of God. This one act of belief and trust not only guaranteed him God's safekeeping but also secured the throne for David and his descendents, including the reign of the coming Messiah who would come from the seed of David.

Saul had been given a similar test when Samuel instructed him to go to Gilgal and wait seven days for him. Samuel told him when he arrived he would sacrifice the peace offering and then he would tell him what he should do.[7] Seven days had passed. The warriors were getting restless and had begun to scatter. Rather than believing God's word and trusting God in spite of the loss of his men, Saul took matters into his own hands. Without regard for Samuel and his high priestly office, Saul made himself a priest and offered the sacrifice.[8] Saul's confidence was in the strength of man to bring victory. In the face of losing what he saw as his arm of strength, he panicked. He determined to save his own life one way or the other. David, on the other hand, was willing to put his life in the hands of God. He ate God's provision with total regard for the priestly position. David didn't seek the strength of men to see him through; he yielded himself to the purpose and plans of God. Saul acted out of his fear, David out of his faith.

God told Saul through the prophet Samuel that his obedience and faith in God's strength would have guaranteed him the kingdom:

> *And Samuel said to Saul, "You have acted foolishly; you have not kept the commandment of the Lord your God, which He commanded you, for now the Lord would have established your kingdom over Israel forever. But now your kingdom shall not endure. The Lord has sought out for Himself a man after His own heart, and the Lord has appointed him as ruler over His people, because you have not kept what the Lord commanded you."[9]*

What a contrast to the end result for David's house:

> *Do you not know that the Lord God of Israel gave the rule over Israel forever to David and his sons by a covenant of salt?[10]*

David not only solidified the family rule of the kingdom in this daring act of faith, but also acquired the position of guardian and protector of the priesthood. In I Samuel 22 we read the account of Saul's reaction to Ahimelech's assistance of David. Doeg the Edomite who was the chief of Saul's shepherds happened to be at the Tabernacle when David had come. Saul's insecurity and jealousy caused him to distrust everyone. In an effort to demonstrate his allegiance to Saul, Doeg told the king what he had witnessed on the night David fled. Saul brought Ahimelech and his sons to give an account. Although Ahimelech accurately informed the king of his ignorance of David's flight, Saul was blinded by his own envy and apprehension. Saul had the priests before him killed, as well as all the priests, their families, and their animals in Nob. Only Abiathar, one of Ahimelech's sons escaped, taking the ephod with him. When he came to David, David took total responsibility for this devastating outcome and pledged protection to him. From that day on, David had an unusual relationship with the priesthood. Several times the ephod Abiathar brought with him played an important part in David's life. When David had to make major decisions regarding Saul's plots against him, he had Abiathar bring the ephod so he could consult God.[11] We see David wearing the ephod as he danced his way into Jerusalem before the ark of the covenant of the Lord.[12]

David had much in common with the priesthood. Both were placed in their positions through the anointing of God and both had their provisions established through a salt covenant. When God gave the Aaronic priesthood (which is different than the Levitical priesthood) their portion, He said to them:

All the offerings of the holy gifts, which the sons of Israel offer to the Lord, I have given to you and your sons and your daughters with you, as a perpetual allotment. It is an everlasting covenant of salt before the Lord to you and your descendants with you. [13]

David had eaten at the table of God, the consecrated priestly table. As a result, there was a special bond David had with the priesthood. Had others tried to mimic David's actions, putting on the ephod and prancing around in priestly apparel, they surely would have regretted it. When someone sat down to a salt covenant meal, they entered into relationship with all partakers. David's courageous act not only bound him to God, it bound him to the priesthood. When David donned the priestly ephod and danced before the ark as it entered Jerusalem, neither Zadok nor Abithar, high priests in the time of David, instructed him to take it off. David certainly was not about to endanger the success of this second attempt to bringing the ark to Jerusalem. David was well aware that the actions of the priests were crucial to this mission.

> *Then David called for Zadok and Abiathar the priests, and for the Levites, for Uriel, Asaiah, Joel Shemaiah, Eliel, and Amminadab, and said to them, "You are the heads of the fathers' household of the Levites; consecrate yourselves both you and your relatives that you may bring up the ark of the Lord God of Israel, to the place that I have prepared for it. Because you did not carry it at the first, the Lord our God made an outburst on us, for we did not seek Him according to the ordinance."*[14]

David knew he had the right to walk before God in the place of a priestly king. What gave him such confidence? David had eaten the priestly bread and had been accepted by God. He was not only in covenant with God but with all those who were represented at the table, a table consecrated only for priests!

Assuredly, no one understood all the dynamics of a salt covenant more than David, the priestly king!

Scripture References

[1] I Samuel 19:1-10
[2] I Samuel 19:11-24
[3] I Samuel 20
[4] Mark 2:25-26
[5] Leviticus 10:1-3
[6] I Samuel 21:1-6
[7] I Samuel 10:8
[8] I Samuel 13:5-10

Please Pass The Salt

[9] I Samuel 13:13-14
[10] II Chronicles 13:5
[11] I Samuel 23:9-12
[12] I Chronicles 15:25-29
[13] Numbers 18:19
[14] I Chronicles 15:12-13

Chapter 4

A Dinner to Remember

*For I received from the Lord
that which I also delivered to you, that the Lord Jesus
in the night in which he was betrayed took bread;
and when He had given thanks,
He broke it, and said,
"This is My body, which is for you;
do this in remembrance of Me."
I Corinthians 11:23-24*

Dr. Shirley M. Carpenter

Chapter 4

A Dinner To Remember!

Friendship Bread

As we look at the salt covenant of the Old Testament, we need to ask ourselves, "What does this have to do with us in this present day?" The answer is found as we read I Corinthians 11:23-24:

> *For I received from the Lord that which I also delivered to you, that the Lord Jesus in the night in which He was betrayed took bread; and when He had given thanks, He broke it, and said, "This is My body, which is for you; do this in remembrance of Me."*

The bread Jesus held in His hand was not ordinary bread. This was not just an ordinary night with a few guests over for a social visit. Jesus brought His disciples together to commemorate Passover. As they sat at the ancient covenant meal, Jesus brought new significance to its elements. We have often marveled at the meaning of the cup, aware of its representation as the new covenant in His blood, but rarely have we been overwhelmed by the wonder of the bread.

The significance of the bread was so vital that this festival also was called The Feast of Unleavened Bread. God chose to demonstrate His commitment as their protector and provider, their friend, by having His people eat the covenant bread for seven days.[1]

On this memorial night, Jesus made it clear to His followers that by His death and the shedding of His blood He would wash away their sins. Likewise, He affirmed that through His death and the sacrificing of His flesh He afforded them the same protection and provision the Israelites had as they left Egypt.

It is not a mere coincidence that on this night of all nights Jesus said to his disciples,

> *"Greater love has no one than this, that one lay down his life for his friends. You are My friends, if you do what I command you. No longer do I call you slaves for the slave does not know what his master is doing; but I have called you friends, for all things that I have heard from My Father I have made known to you."*[2]

Jesus knew the work of the cross would not only establish the blood covenant for His followers, but also the friendship covenant. His great desire once again, is not only to be our savior, but to be our friend. His provision does not merely prepare us for eternity, but provides for our earthly necessities as well. Just as God promised to sustain and defend the Israelites, He pledges to meet our needs, and fight our battles.

You Be The Judge

Paul tells us about the night Jesus set this table of communion in order:

> *For I received from the Lord that which I also delivered to you, that the Lord Jesus in the night in which He was betrayed took bread; and when He had given thanks, He broke it, and said, "This is My body, which is for you; do this in remembrance of Me." In the same way He took the cup also, after supper, saying, "This cup is the new covenant in My blood; do this, as often as you drink it, in remembrance of Me." For as often as you eat this bread and drink this cup, you proclaim the Lord's death until He comes. Therefore, whoever eats the bread or drinks the cup of the Lord in an unworthy manner, shall be guilty of the body and the blood of the Lord. But let a man examine himself and so let him eat of the bread and drink of the cup. For he who eats and drinks, eats and drinks judgment to himself, if he does not judge the body rightly.*[3]

Caution is given to those who participate in this covenant meal. Proper preparation is a must and recollection is an essential part of the process. To insure a suitable self-examination as well as a thorough body inspection we need to look at the heart of Passover and its relevance to the believer today. After Jesus had gathered His apostles and they were reclining at the table, Jesus made an enlightening statement:

> *I have earnestly desired to eat this Passover with you before I suffer; for I say to you, I shall never again eat it until it is fulfilled in the kingdom of God.*[4]

Jesus made it clear that His death on the cross was the fulfillment of the slaying of the Passover lamb, but Passover itself would not be complete until it was "fulfilled in the kingdom of God." To understand this statement, we must go back to the first Passover and remember the purpose of the blood. Exodus 12:21-24 says:

> *Then Moses called for all the elders of Israel, and said to them, "Go and take for yourselves lambs according to your families, and slay the Passover lamb. And you shall take a bunch of hyssop and dip it in the blood which is in the basin, and apply some of the blood that is in the basin to the lintel and the two doorposts; and none of you shall go outside the door of his house until morning. For the Lord will pass through to smite the Egyptians; and when He sees the blood on the lintel and the two doorposts, the Lord will pass over the door and will not allow the destroyer to come in your houses to smite you. And you shall observe this event as an ordinance for you and your children forever.*

The blood was to keep "death" from having any affect on them. When will this be fulfilled in God's kingdom? Truly every believer has the blood applied to the door of their heart and has been given the promise of eternal life. But if Jesus doesn't come back within a given number of years, we all will die. The answer to our question is found when we read Revelation 20:11-15 (emphasis is mine).

And I saw a great white throne and Him who sat upon it, from whose presence earth and heaven fled away, and no place was found for them. And I saw the dead, the great and the small standing before the throne, and books were opened; and another book was opened, which is the book of life; and the dead were judged from the things which were written in the books, according to their deeds. And the sea gave up the dead which were in it, and death and Hades gave up the dead which were in them; and they were judged everyone of them according to their deeds. And death and Hades were thrown into the lake of fire. **This is the second death,** *the lake of fire. And if anyone's name was not found written in the book of life, he was thrown into the lake of fire.*

Revelation 13:8 refers to "the book of life" as "the book of life of the Lamb who has been slain." Every name in the book is protected by the blood of the slain Lamb. As surely as death took every firstborn of Egypt who was not protected under the blood of the Passover lamb, the second death will swallow up everyone who is not sheltered under the shed blood of Jesus, the Lamb who takes away the sin of the world. Jesus wrote to the faithful who would be martyred in Revelation 2:10-11 and said:

"Do not fear what you are about to suffer. Behold, the devil is about to cast some of you into prison, that you may be tested, and you will have tribulation ten days. Be faithful until death, and I will give you the crown of life. He who has an ear,

let him hear what the Spirit says to the churches. **He who overcomes shall not be hurt by the second death.** (Emphasis is mine).

It is at the time of the "second death" we see Passover completely fulfilled. The blood of Jesus applied to the hearts of the believers will spare us from eternal death. Immediately after this we see the eternal kingdom of Christ set up and His marriage to His Bride take place. Passover has been fulfilled!

Just as the pouring out of His blood resulted in salvation, the breaking of His body also brought about something significant. When Jesus took the bread, He established the picture of His body. Often we hear Isaiah 53:5 read in relationship to the communion table"

But He was pierced through for our transgressions, He was crushed for our iniquities; the chastening for our wellbeing fell upon Him, and by His scourging we are healed.

This passage is often quoted as proof positive that every believer is to experience physical healing. Although I do believe in God's healing power, I believe we have limited the truth of this passage. The Word speaks to us in many different ways. It is not uncommon for the Spirit to quicken the Word to us as individuals, even when the Scripture is written to a nation or a people group. But in so doing, His intent is not to eliminate it's broader interpretation. When God breathed these words, He was speaking to Zion, the people of God.

We can discern Jesus' charge "to discern the body rightly" and the healing effect of the suffering servant of Isaiah 53:5 when we look at the visual message Jesus left on the day He resurrected.

The crucifixion was over. The body of the hoped-for Messiah was carefully sealed in a borrowed tomb. With His death, the hopes and dreams of the disciples died also. There would be no overthrow of the Roman government, no reestablishing of David's rule and authority, no reasons to strive for high military positions. The hands that stretched forth and released the power of the Kingdom of God laid lifeless. The feet that had showed them how to walk had taken their last step. Arms and limbs once alive and energetic were now stiff with paralyzing rigor mortis. Death held the body of Christ in its grip.

The religious leaders of Israel had rejected their king. Roman rule had joined the threat of bringing the Kingdom of God to a perceived end. Peter, James, John and the rest of the disciples, now fearful for their own lives, sought a safe hiding place. The shackles of their guilt and shame were greater prisons than what awaited them if they were found and arrested.

The flabbergasted trio of females who had just scurried in from their angelic encounter at the tomb brought baffling news to the fugitives. "The angel told us He is risen from the dead. The tomb is empty!"

Struggling with shock and disbelief, Peter and John raced to the tomb to check out the message for themselves. John outran Peter but hesitated at the entrance of the sepulcher. Peter pushed passed his comrade's reluctance and entered the burial-chamber.[5] Although they found the grave empty, it was filled with a message regarding the body.

The linen wrappings that had covered his corpse were still lying in the tomb, but the piece that had covered Jesus' head was folded up and placed by itself.[6] Why had Jesus taken time to care for the head piece while leaving the rest of the grave clothes disheveled? The answer seems rather obvious once the riddle is solved. Jesus was leaving them a message. No longer would His body merely consist of His physical frame. From the moment of His resurrection, His body would encompass many members of which He was and is the head.[7] Concerning the Head, His work was done! But the rest of His body still required a bit more work!

The New Testament body of Christ tends to be sickly and in need of the healing stripes of Christ. It is not that the believers who make up His members do not accept Jesus and His work of the cross. The problem is that often we do not accept one another.
Imagine for a moment that I took you home to meet my husband Greg. I take you into the living room and say, "Here on my living room sofa is Greg's head. Please come into the kitchen with me so that you can meet the

rest of him." Arriving in the kitchen, I point out a pair of hands on the kitchen counter and announce, "These are Greg's hands. I have his legs and feet in my bedroom closet and that's his torso laying on the bed." How much would you enjoy meeting my husband Greg? Anyone with a bit of sense would cry out, "Greg, pull yourself together!"

But all too often this is the image of the body of Christ we display to one another and to the world. Believers fight and bicker. They hold resentment and bitterness in their hearts toward each other. They cut off any portion of the body that doesn't embrace their pet methods or man-made doctrines. The world looks at the dismembered, disfigured body of Christ and feels repulsed. Is it any wonder that so many people today prefer to stay as far away from the church, Christ's body, as they can get. Yet it is this love for one another that is to be our very testimony of loving Him.

> "A new commandment I give to you, that you love one another, even as I have loved you, that you also love one another. "By this all men will know that you are My disciples, if you have love for one another."[9]

Preparation for partaking of the communion bread requires an individual to judge **the body**, Christ's New Testament body rightly. The result of failing to do so brings weakness, sickness, and even death to His members.[8]

We understand the reason for the consequences even more when we understand that **each one** represented at a salt-covenant meal is in covenant **with one another**. This salt covenant is not only between God and me, but with every believer who partakes of the same loaf. I Corinthians 10:17 puts it this way:

> *I speak to wise men; you judge what I say. Is not the cup of blessing which we bless a sharing in the blood of Christ? Is not the bread which we break a sharing in the body of Christ? Since there is one bread, we who are many are one body; for we all partake of one bread.*

On the night Jesus inaugurated the New Covenant meal establishing the friendship covenant, He said, *"No longer do I call you slaves; for the slave does not know what his master is doing; but I have called you friends..."*[10] After establishing the covenant with His followers, He went on to bring the awareness that all who sat at the table were in covenant as well. Jesus said, *"This is my commandment, that you love one another, just as I have loved you,"*[11] and, *"You are My friends, if you do what I command you."*[12] Loving one another was to be the sure sign of loving Him.

Like Saul, we have broken the salt-covenant and need it to be reestablished. Restoration only comes through the death of the guilty member, not a physical death, but a dying to self.

God does not tell us to go around judging those in the body; He tells us to judge our own attitude toward His body. I am not responsible for what others think of me, but I am held accountable for what I think of others. Jesus is waiting for us to love His body as He does. When that is reality, we will care for it as He does and fulfill the demands of the salt-covenant.

> ...for no one ever hated his own flesh, but nourishes and cherishes it, just as Christ also does the church, because we are members of His body.[13]

Scripture References

[1] Exodus 12:14-20
[2] John 15:13-15
[3] I Corinthians 11:23-29
[4] Luke 22:15-16
[5] John 20:1-5
[6] John 20:6-7
[7] Ephesians 4:15-16 & I Corinthians 11
[8] I Corinthians 11:29-30
[9] John 13:34-35
[10] John 15:15
[11] John 15:12
[12] John 15:17
[13] Ephesians 5:29-30

Dr. Shirley M. Carpenter

Please Pass The Salt

After Thoughts

Is Anyone Thirsty?

*Salt is good; but if the salt becomes unsalty,
with what will you make it salty again?
Have salt in yourselves,
and be at peace with one another.
Mark 9:50*

Dr. Shirley M. Carpenter

After Thoughts

Is Anyone Thirsty?

Salt has the quality of creating thirst. Once again the spiritual parallel becomes evident as we examine the results of God's love and care in our lives. When we see His hand of provision and protection, it makes us love and desire Him more.

Jesus told us, *"You are the salt of the earth; but if the salt has become tasteless, how will it be made salty again? It is good for nothing any more, except to be thrown out and trampled underfoot by men."*[1]

Like the farmer who puts out the salt lick to cause the cattle to become thirsty, God has called us to be salt in the world. Our love for people, both in the world and in the body of Christ, can cause others to thirst for the Living Water or turn from Him.

God promised that every life will be touched with salt,

For Everyone will be salted with fire,[2]

The fire of God can either ignite us with His light and life so that we have an effect on those we come in contact with, or it can consume and destroy us. A constant walk with God can turn us into heavenly salt licks, causing our world to thirst after the Living God.

Salt has an amazing affect on ice. When we lived in the Detroit area, the roads were sprinkled with salt to melt the ice and snow in the winter. Unfortunately, I've met some people whose hearts were colder than a Detroit highway in an ice storm. God has given us the substance that will defrost their inward parts and leave them sensitive toward God.

Salt doesn't always have a pleasant impact. Pouring salt in a wound can seem like a cruel thing to do, but it can be just what a person needs. Its antiseptic qualities can ward off infection and promote healing. Solomon said it this way, *"Better is open rebuke than love that is concealed. Faithful are the wounds of a friend, but deceitful are the kisses of an enemy."*[3] There are times we have to go beyond the fear that the salt we bring may cause pain. If we know that, in the end, it will bring healing we must run the risk and pour in the salt.

Everyone needs salt to live, to spice up their lives, to have healthy bodies. We've got the salt the world really needs! This salt was paid for by the blood Jesus shed, the sweat that poured from Him in the garden as He prayed, and the tears He shed for all of mankind. The salt, His salt is between us.

May the reality of the salt covenant between God and His people encourage each believer to trust Him more. It is my earnest prayer that the awareness of the salt covenant between each one who makes up the body of Christ will give us the ability to look beyond each other's faults and differences and see the life of

Jesus in each member.

The salt covenant obligates us to be there when our brother or sister is in need and protect each other when a part of the body is under attack. When the family of God walks together in unity it will bring the reality of the anointing on the church.

> *Behold how good and how pleasant it is for brothers to dwell together in unity! It is like the precious oil upon the head, coming down upon the beard, even Aaron's beard, coming down upon the edges of his robes.*[4]

The next time we sit at the communion table, may we hold the bread in our hand and with a heart of love declare to God, as well as all those who partake of the same loaf,

"THE SALT IS BETWEEN US!"

And may we sense the hungry craving of the world as it cries out for the reality of God. Their actions are pleading,

"PLEASE PASS THE SALT!"

Scripture References
[1] Mark 9:49
[2] Matthew 5:13
[3] Proverbs 27:5-6
[4] Psalm 133:1-2

Dr. Shirley M. Carpenter

Other Books and Publications by Carpenter Ministries

BOOKS

A Rock Garden Locked

From Glory to Glory
or
Through The Knothole By The Nose

Closer Than A Brother

Fit For A King

In The Cool of the Day

BOOKLETS

Our Father

The Last Word

Won't You Be My Neighbor
or
Why Did The Chickens Cross the Road

For more information please contact

Carpenter Ministries
www. carpenterministries.org

Made in the USA
San Bernardino, CA
13 January 2019